THOUGHTFUL THINKERS

7 powerful affirmations
for children & adults

Roochi Sahi

D1743688

All rights reserved Copyright © Roochi Sahi, 2020

The right of Roochi Sahi to be identified as the author of this work has been asserted in accordance with Section 78 of the Copyright, Designs and Patents Act 1988

The book cover is copyright to Roochi Sahi

This book is published by Grosvenor House Publishing Ltd Link House 140 The Broadway, Tolworth, Surrey, KT6 7HT.
www.grosvenorhousepublishing.co.uk

This book is sold subject to the conditions that it shall not, by way of trade or otherwise, be lent, resold, hired out or otherwise circulated without the author's or publisher's prior consent in any form of binding or cover other than that in which it is published and without a similar condition including this condition being imposed on the subsequent purchaser.

A CIP record for this book is available from the British Library

ISBN 978-1-83975-190-5

For Kiana & Mio

Love you to infinity

Thoughts become things

"
I
CAN DO
or
BE ANYTHING
I put my mind to
"

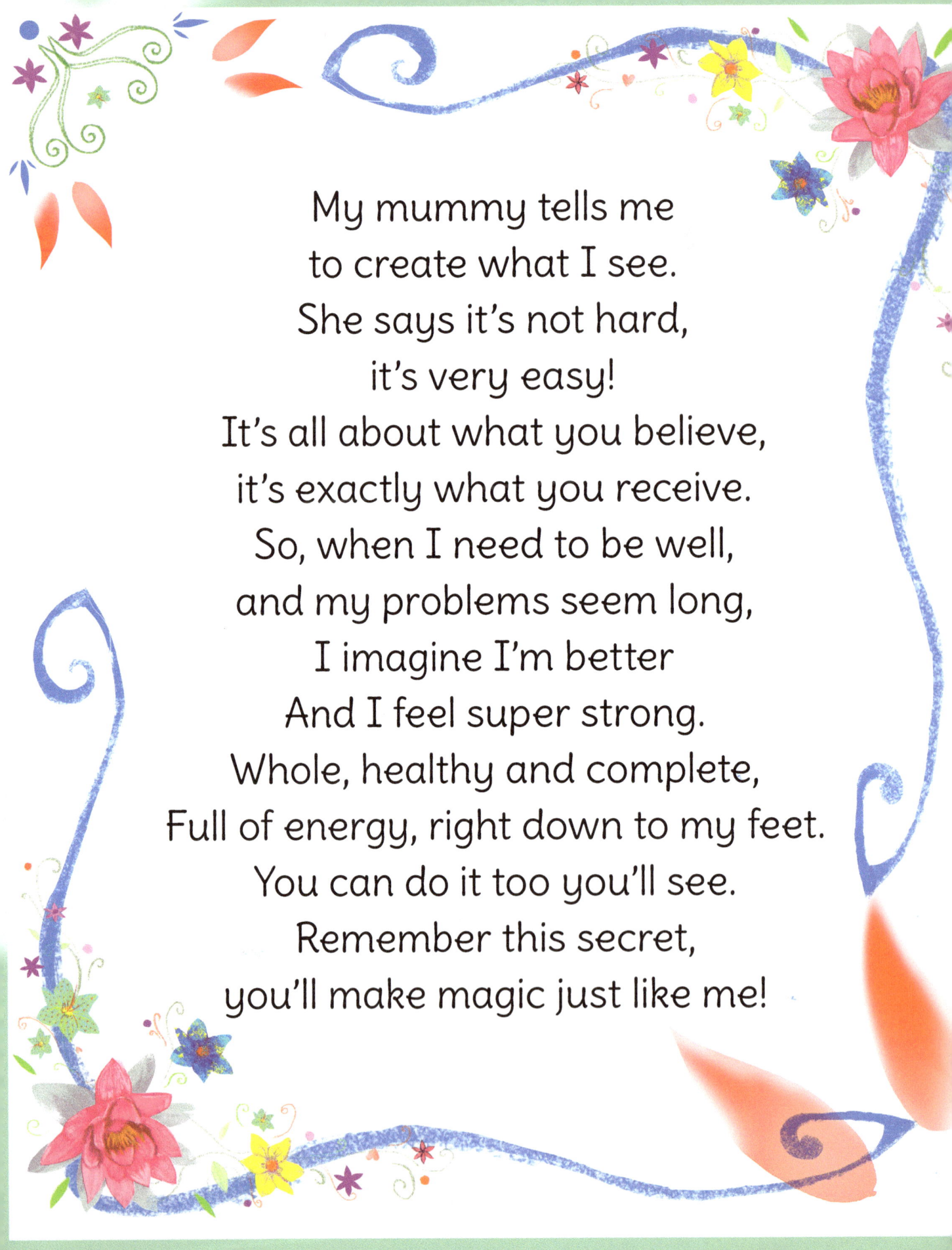

My mummy tells me
to create what I see.
She says it's not hard,
it's very easy!
It's all about what you believe,
it's exactly what you receive.
So, when I need to be well,
and my problems seem long,
I imagine I'm better
And I feel super strong.
Whole, healthy and complete,
Full of energy, right down to my feet.
You can do it too you'll see.
Remember this secret,
you'll make magic just like me!

The super power of Smiling

"

Only
GOOD THINGS
happen to me

"

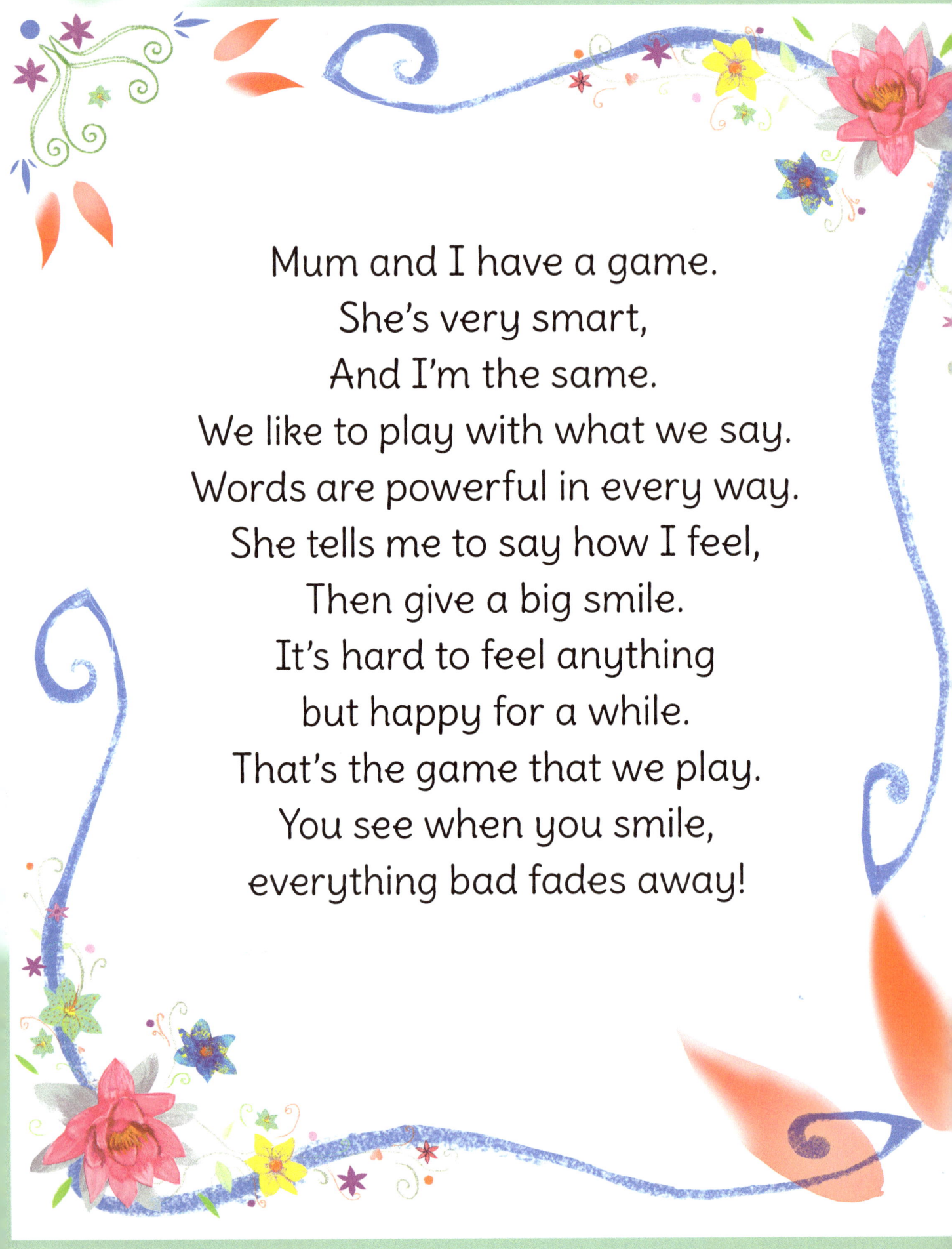

Mum and I have a game.
She's very smart,
And I'm the same.
We like to play with what we say.
Words are powerful in every way.
She tells me to say how I feel,
Then give a big smile.
It's hard to feel anything
but happy for a while.
That's the game that we play.
You see when you smile,
everything bad fades away!

Your Angel Within

" I am always
LOVED "

My mother told me,
About a fairy who sits on my knee.
She's an angel with wings,
And probably sings.
She may look like a friend that I know,
Or it could even be a He,
with pretty pink toes!
There is one thing that I know for sure,
Asking your angel is exactly the cure.
When you need anything,
Just give your very own Angel a ring.
There's no need to hide,
Because you will soon see,
You are actually the true Angel inside!

Create what you want

"
I AM
that
I AM
"

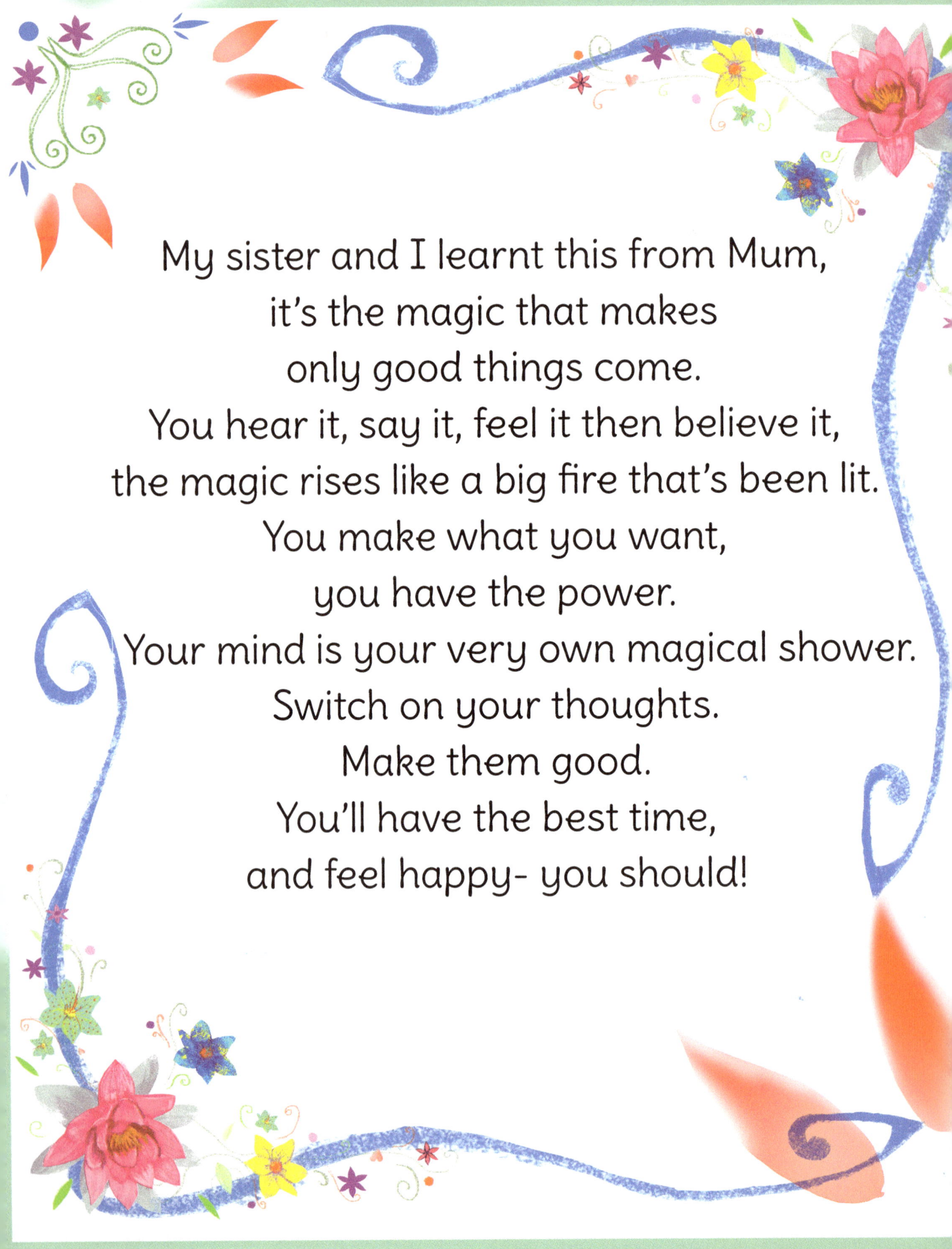

My sister and I learnt this from Mum,
it's the magic that makes
only good things come.
You hear it, say it, feel it then believe it,
the magic rises like a big fire that's been lit.
You make what you want,
you have the power.
Your mind is your very own magical shower.
Switch on your thoughts.
Make them good.
You'll have the best time,
and feel happy- you should!

Let it go and be free

"

I FORGIVE myself

"

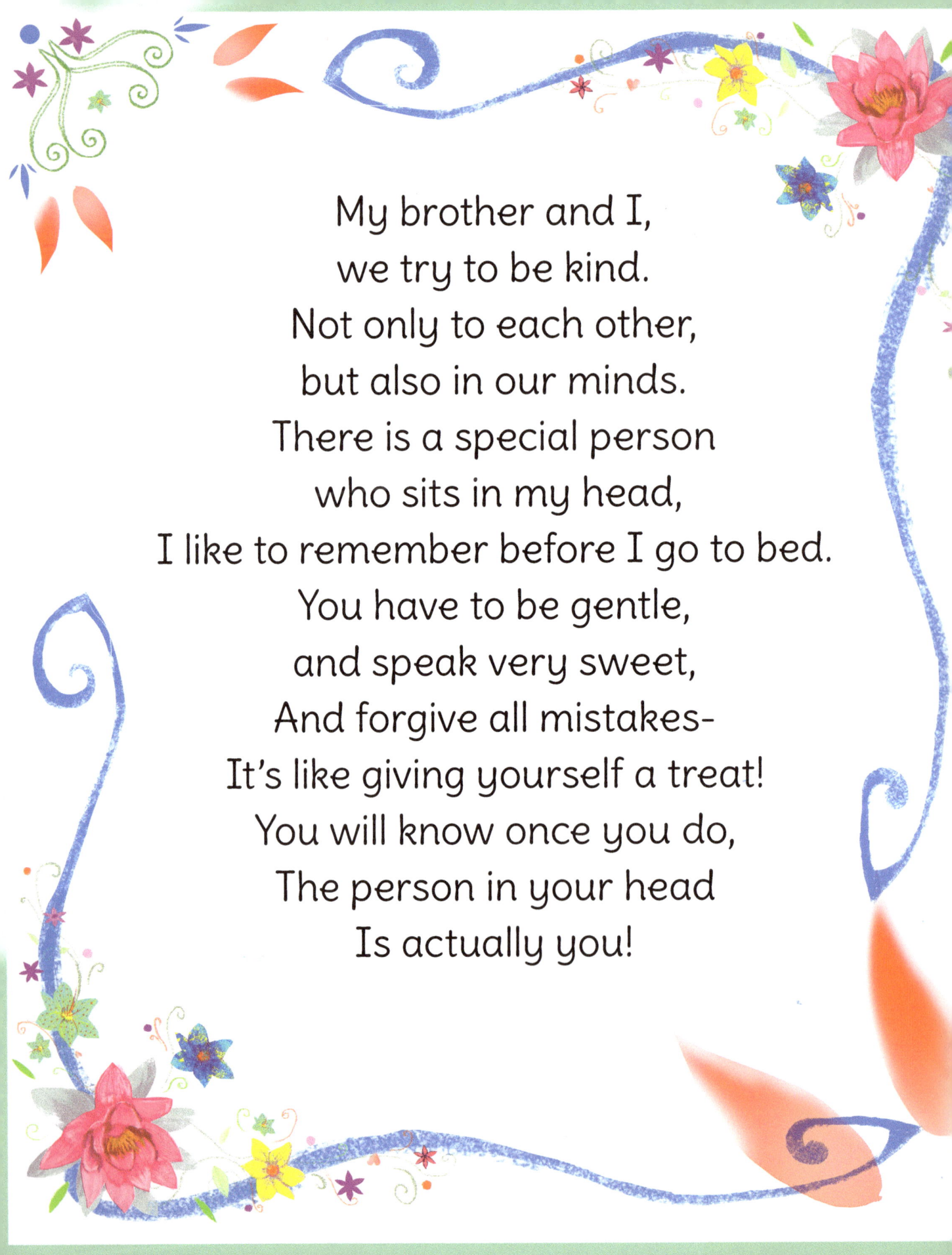

My brother and I,
we try to be kind.
Not only to each other,
but also in our minds.
There is a special person
who sits in my head,
I like to remember before I go to bed.
You have to be gentle,
and speak very sweet,
And forgive all mistakes-
It's like giving yourself a treat!
You will know once you do,
The person in your head
Is actually you!

The Grateful are the greatest

" I am THANKFUL "

My mum told me what gets you more.
It's not crying and screaming
that's for sure.
It's saying thank you
- I promise its true.
When you are grateful,
everything will come to you.
So never look at things and feel sad,
See through your eyes how life isn't bad.
You have so much to say "thank you" for,
with your heart,
Do it, and watch it turn into more,
it's a joyful art!

How to love you

" I LOVE Myself "

There is one more important message
I must not forget.
You are the only person
that you can protect.
Your mind, your heart,
They have been yours since the start.
You must love You and mustn't feel blue.
This is the best way, it's very true.

Notes from the Author:

I was born in America, in the state o[f] Philadelphia. When I was three years old[,] my family moved to Africa- and Keny[a] was where I spent most of my childhood[.] Engulfed in a world of beautiful climate[,] wildlife, beaches and exceptional nature[,] I organically grew poetic in my mind. M[y] environment nurtured my developmen[t] and both my parents being Dentists, I wa[s] inspired by them to study Dentistry. Jumpin[g] from a life surrounded by nature, I moved t[o] the bustling city of London; to establish my education, and thi[s] put my imagination into context with my new London reality.

A fully qualified Dentist, I went on to gain post-graduat[e] qualifications in Aesthetic Medicine. Alongside this academi[c] but scientific upbringing, I was always fascinated with Holisti[c] Health. After completing a study of Hypnotherapy and gainin[g] qualifications in Complementary Medicine, I changed a great dea[l] in my life, and later became a mother of two beautiful childre[n.] As a result of these combined experiences, I became the founder o[f] an empowering mindfulness system, called 'Dr. By Roochi', wher[e] 'Discover Radiance' uses a method of subconscious programmin[g] in adults to create powerful and positive beliefs.

My books for children work with a similar methodology- and what better way to help children form such pathways for thought; so that they can begin to achieve, create, learn and understand their own capabilities as early as possible.

My books aim to encourage the practice of mindfulness for children as young as 2 years old and help them cope with both imaginative interpretation and emotion as they evolve.

My mother has believed in my ability as a Children's book author since as long as I can remember. Always forging on with the waves of life I always had an excuse to why it was never the right time. Until the tide went out, and now, here I am, writing books that have truly come from my heart.

My books, like countless ventures in my life, reflect the utmost gratitude to my supportive and loving family. Thank you for everything, Dad, Mum and my best friend- my husband.

With Love, Light and Laughter always,

Roochi Sahi

You can follow my updates on
Facebook & Instagram: dr.byroochi

W: www.drbyroochi.com

dr.
BY ROOCHI

Lightning Source UK Ltd.
Milton Keynes UK
UKHW050529271020
372264UK00003B/121